Did you know...
Animal Edition

Find out more about your favourite animals around the world.

Bring color to their homes as the characters show you their favourite places and things to do!

Allo, I'm Melvin the tortoise! Did you know...

My shell is made up of 60 different bones!

I can smell my yummy food with my throat,

and I can live for a really, really long time. Maybe even 190 years!

Let me show you my home!

I love napping under the palm trees at my home!

The sound of the waves crashing are sooo relaxing

The sun is always shining during the day!

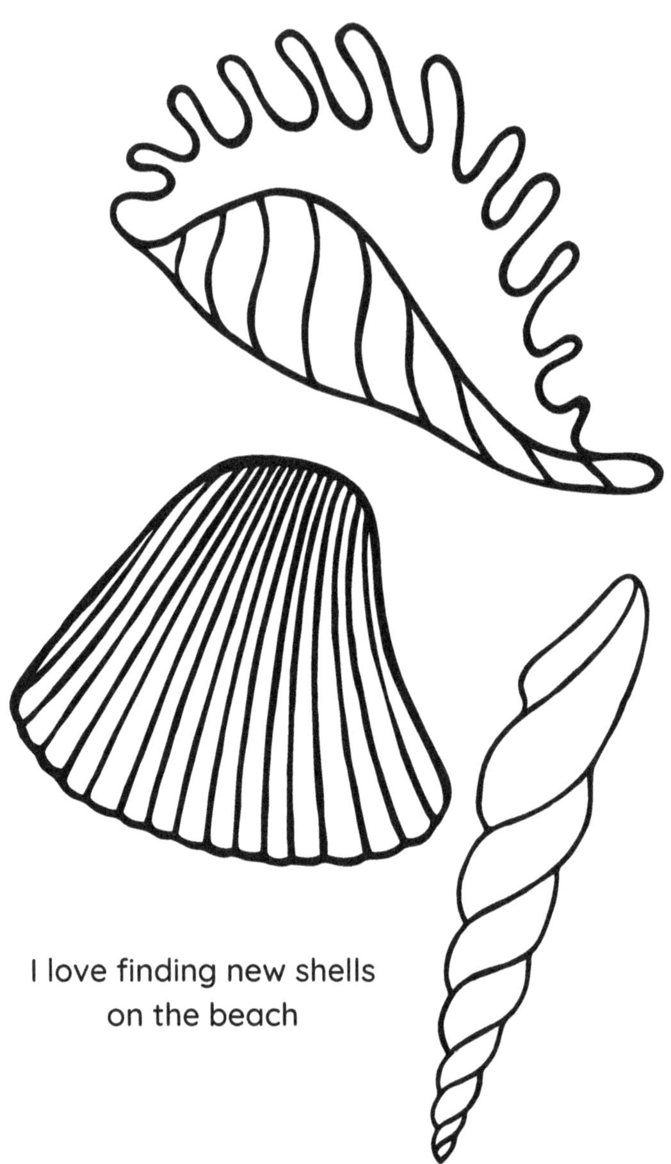

I love finding new shells
on the beach

Hi, I'm Chuck the walrus! Did you know...

My big teeth are called 'tusks',

they can grow up to 90cm long when i'm older.

I can also sleep underwater!

Let me show my home!

I spend a lot of time in the ocean!

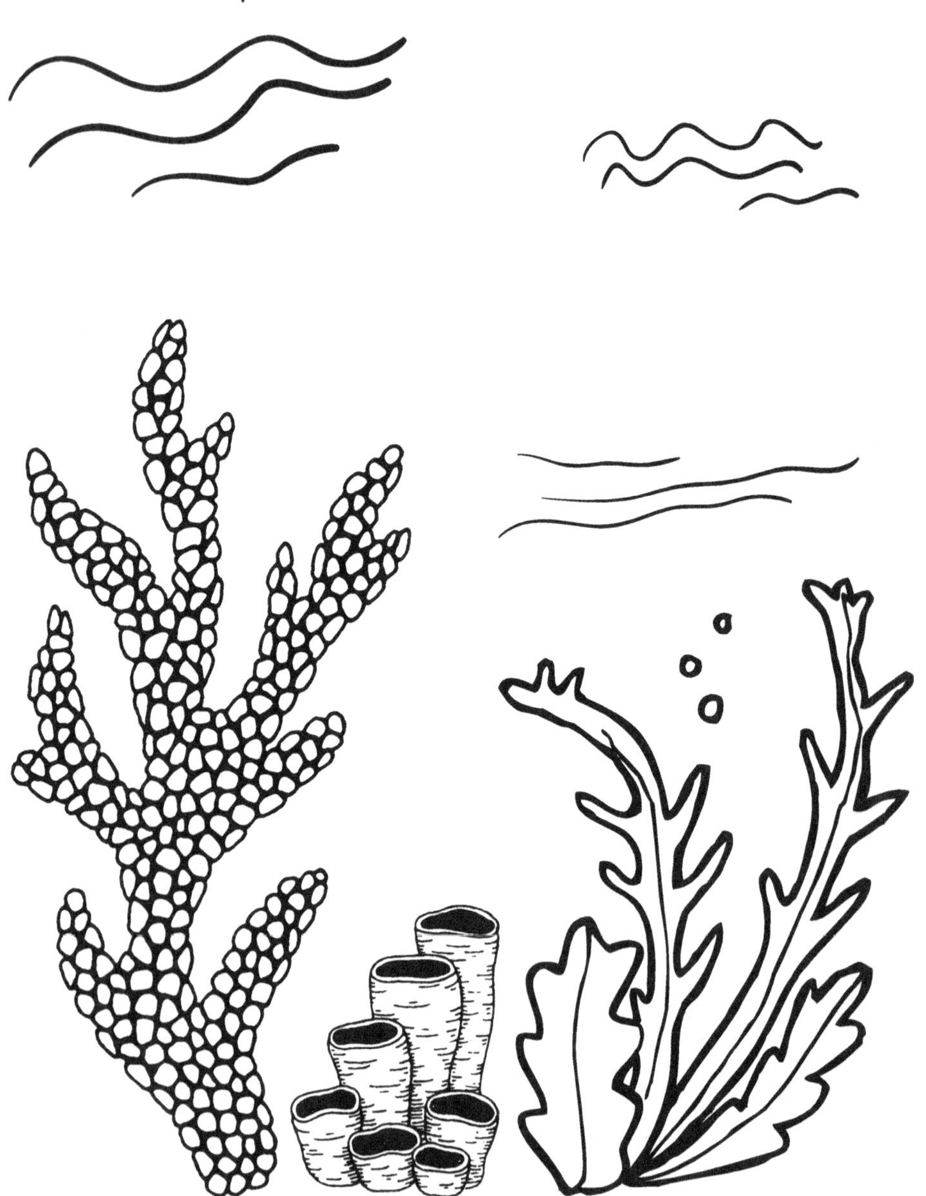

Meet my friends!

Sometimes there's beautiful mountains to look at!

...and so many fish!

Hallo, I'm Tabby the Ostrich!
Did you know...

When I'm all grown, I could be almost 9 feet tall!

I may not be able to fly, but I can run really fast.

I don't have teeth, so i swallow stones to help grind up my food!

Let me show you my home!

My my friend!

We have awesome waterfalls!

So many pretty flowers!

During the spring, all the babies are born!

G'day, I'm Mirrie the koala!
Did you know...

I'm nocturnal, which means I sleep in the day and play at night!

My all time favourite food is eucalyptus leaves.

Because I'm a girl, I only have up to one baby per year.

Let me show you my home!

Mmm... My favourite food!

Here is a didgeridoo and a boomerang!

Here's some of my friends!

Oooh... The Sydney Opera House.

Salama, I'm Rocco the chameleon! Did you know...

I have color changing skin that makes me an expert at 'hide and seek'

I can move my eyes in two different directions at the same time!

My tongue can be as long as my whole body. Crazy!

Let me show my home!

This is my friend!

I love my rainforest home

The night sky is so beuatiful!

I love waving to Mr Corocodile!

Did you know...
Animal Edition

Live Optimal Publishing
2021

Author: Shanie Sellar
Illustrations: various contributors